THE LITTLE
INSTRUCTION
BOOK FOR
DOGS

THE LITTLE INSTRUCTION BOOK FOR DOGS

This revised edition copyright © Summersdale Publishers Ltd, 2018
First published in 2014

Research by Malcolm Croft

Illustrations by Dannyboy

An Hachette UK Company
www.hachette.co.uk

Summersdale Publishers Ltd
Part of Octopus Publishing Group Limited
Carmelite House
50 Victoria Embankment
LONDON
EC4Y 0DZ

www.summersdale.com

Printed and bound in China

ISBN: 978-1-78685-533-6

Substantial discounts on bulk quantities of Summersdale books are available to corporations, professional associations and other organisations. For details contact general enquiries: telephone: +44 (0) 1243 771107 or email: enquiries@summersdale.com.

THE LITTLE
INSTRUCTION
BOOK FOR
DOGS

CARRYING STICKS TEN TIMES THE SIZE OF YOUR
OWN BODY IS ADMIRABLE, IF NOT PRACTICAL

DANNYBOY
AND **KATE FREEMAN**

summersdale

If you think dogs can't count, try putting
three dog biscuits in your pocket and
then give him only two of them.

PHIL PASTORET

INTRODUCTION

People think a dog's life is easy: you get to lick yourself clean, somebody else picks up your poo, you're fed continuously (because you'll eat anything), and you get your very own personal trainer taking you out for exercise (without having to pay a monthly gym membership). But the truth is, being a dog is actually very hard work. And there's no instruction manual for how to be a good dog either – you just have to make it up as you go along… until now.

This book is your ultimate companion to becoming a better dog – not a good dog, or a less bad dog – but better; a dog that deserves its own place at (the head of) the family dinner table, not underneath it.

INSTRUCTION NO. 1

SLIPPERS ARE MEANT TO BE CHEWED.
DON'T FEEL BAD ABOUT IT — IT SEEMS
TO REALLY EXCITE THE HUMANS.

INSTRUCTION No. 2

SQUEAKY TOYS. BEST SQUEAKED
REPEATEDLY AT 4 A.M.

INSTRUCTION No. 3

THE OPTIMUM VIEWPOINT FOR ROAD
TRIPS IS THE DRIVER'S LAP.

INSTRUCTION No. 4

THE GOLDEN RULE WHEN IT COMES TO SNIFFING
DOGS' BOTTOMS IS: DON'T SNIFF A DOG'S BOTTOM
IF THAT DOG IS CURRENTLY SNIFFING ANOTHER
DOG'S BOTTOM. IT ALL GETS VERY CONFUSING.

INSTRUCTION No. 5

DOG LEADS ARE SILLY INVENTIONS. SHOW YOUR
HUMAN JUST HOW INCONVENIENT THEY ARE BY
RUNNING IN CIRCLES AROUND AND BETWEEN
THEIR LEGS – AND AROUND AND BETWEEN
OTHER PEOPLE'S LEGS, TOO.

INSTRUCTION No.6

IF YOU'RE GOING TO GO DIGGING UP FLOWER BEDS
IN THE BACK YARD WHILE LOOKING FOR BONES,
ENSURE THAT IT IS THE MOST RECENTLY PLANTED
FLOWER BED TO PROVIDE MAXIMUM DRAMA.

INSTRUCTION No.7

DOG POO. YOU MAY HAVE HUNDREDS
OF THOUSANDS OF YEARS OF EVOLUTION
TELLING YOU THAT YOU NEED TO EAT IT.
BUT YOU DON'T. YOU REALLY DON'T.

INSTRUCTION NO. 8

WAGGING YOUR TAIL IS A GREAT WAY
TO COMMUNICATE WITH HUMANS, SO
DO IT ENTHUSIASTICALLY AND OFTEN.
BONUS: THE MORE THINGS YOU KNOCK
OVER WITH YOUR TAIL, THE MORE
EXCITED YOUR HUMAN BECOMES.

INSTRUCTION No. 9

WASHING MACHINES ARE NOT TELEVISIONS.

WHENEVER THERE IS A BABY OR SMALL CHILD AROUND, LOITER NEARBY. THEY CAN'T HOLD THINGS VERY WELL SO TEND TO DROP LOTS OF FOOD SCRAPS ON THE FLOOR. HELP BY CLEARING THEM UP BEFORE THE HUMANS CAN.

INSTRUCTION No.11

ALWAYS REMEMBER THE OLD DOGGY ADAGE,
''TIS BETTER TO HAVE EATEN SOMETHING,
THROWN IT UP AND EATEN IT AGAIN, THAN
NEVER TO HAVE EATEN IT IN THE FIRST PLACE.'

INSTRUCTION No.12

THE MORE EXPENSIVE THE NEW DOG BED, THE
MORE APPEALING THE HARD FLOOR BECOMES.

INSTRUCTION No. 13

YOU GET LOTS OF TREATS WHEN YOUR HUMANS
ARE TRYING TO TRAIN YOU TO DO NEW TRICKS.
SURE, YOU CAN DO THE TRICK, BUT WHY WOULD
YOU LET THEM THINK THEY CAN STOP WITH THE
TREATS? ACT DUMB UNTIL YOU'VE HAD YOUR FILL.

INSTRUCTION NO. 14

HOWLING IS FUN, NO MATTER THE OCCASION,
BUT IT CAN BE USED TO YOUR ADVANTAGE
IF YOUR HUMANS LOOK LIKE THEY'RE
ABOUT TO LEAVE THE HOUSE WITHOUT
YOU. THEY WON'T LEAVE FOR FEAR YOU'LL
UPSET THE NEIGHBOURS, GIVING YOU AN
EXTRA 10 MINUTES OF ATTENTION.

INSTRUCTION No. 15

THE QUICKER YOU EAT THE FOOD YOUR
HUMANS GIVE YOU, THE QUICKER THEY'LL
REPLACE IT. THIS THEORY HAS NEVER
ACTUALLY BEEN PROVEN, BUT WE KNOW OUR
HUMANS THINK WE'RE STARVING REALLY.
SO WOLF IT DOWN LIKE A GOOD DOG.

INSTRUCTION No.16

HUMANS WILL ALWAYS BLAME THEIR
FARTS ON YOU. DON'T TAKE IT LYING
DOWN. GET YOUR OWN BACK.

INSTRUCTION No. 17

LONG, MUDDY WALKS IN THE RAIN ARE GREAT. PROLONG THE SENSORY EXPERIENCE FOR YOU AND THE FAMILY BY TRAIPSING AROUND THE HOUSE, SHAKING OFF MUD EVERYWHERE AND RUBBING THE SMELL INTO THE CARPET FOR EVERYONE TO ENJOY.

INSTRUCTION No.18

THE HOOVER MAY BE NOISY
BUT IT IS NOT YOUR ENEMY.

INSTRUCTION No. 19

PERFECT YOUR BEST HANGDOG EXPRESSION
TO BRING OUT IN EMERGENCIES: EXTREME
HUNGER, BEING PUT OUT IN THE YARD IN
THE RAIN, WHEN THERE'S STEAK JUST OUT
OF REACH, OR WHEN IN DIRE NEED OF
A BEHIND-THE-EAR SCRATCH.

INSTRUCTION No. 20

ALWAYS DRINK FROM THE TOILET. IF IT
WASN'T MEANT FOR DRINKING, WHY DID
THEY MAKE IT TASTE SO DELICIOUS?

INSTRUCTION No. 21

AN OPEN DISHWASHER IS AN INVITATION TO LICK
CLEAN ALL THE PLATES, BOWLS AND CUTLERY.

INSTRUCTION No. 22

HOSEPIPES. FRIEND OR FOE? YOU CAN'T BE SURE. KEEP A WARY EYE ON THEM AND KEEP YOUR DISTANCE, JUST TO BE SAFE.

INSTRUCTION No. 23

THE MOMENT SOMEONE TRIES TO
TAKE A NICE PICTURE OF YOU IS THE
PERFECT TIME TO HAVE A POO.

INSTRUCTION No. 24

LEARN TO OPEN DOORS WITH YOUR PAWS. THAT
WAY YOU'LL NEVER BE FAR FROM THE ACTION.

INSTRUCTION No. 25

HUMANS ARE MESSY CREATURES, AND
SOMETIMES THEY GET FOOD AROUND THEIR
FACES, IN THEIR BEARDS, OR ON THEIR HANDS.
HELP THEM OUT BY LICKING IT OFF.

IT'S IMPORTANT THAT YOU HUMP ANYTHING AND EVERYTHING, TO ASSERT YOUR DOMINANCE AROUND THE HOUSE. THIS INCLUDES SOFT TOYS, CUSHIONS, FURNITURE LEGS AND HUMAN LEGS (ESPECIALLY THOSE BELONGING TO MOTHERS-IN-LAW).

BEING LEFT ALONE IS UNACCEPTABLE, AND YOUR HUMANS NEED TO LEARN THAT. THE BEST WAY TO GET THE MESSAGE ACROSS IS BY DESTROYING AS MUCH OF THE HOUSE AS YOU CAN IF THEY LEAVE YOU FOR MORE THAN FIVE MINUTES. THAT WAY THEY'LL BE TOO SCARED TO EVER LEAVE THE HOUSE AGAIN.

INSTRUCTION No. 28

WHENEVER YOU HEAR BATHWATER
RUNNING, YOU MUST CHARGE AROUND THE
HOUSE IN A FLURRY OF FUR AND PANIC
TO AVOID ANY RISK OF BEING CAUGHT
AND DUMPED INTO THE AWFUL, HORRIBLE,
DISGUSTINGLY FRESH-SMELLING WATER.

IF YOU FEEL YOUR HUMAN IS MORE
INTERESTED IN THEIR PHONE OR TABLET
THAN IN PETTING YOU, KNOCKING A GLASS
OF WATER OVER ONTO THE SCREEN WHEN
THEY NEXT LEAVE IT LYING AROUND IS A
SURE-FIRE WAY TO GET THEIR ATTENTION.

INSTRUCTION No. 30

AS ONE OF THE MOST LOYAL CREATURES ON EARTH, YOUR FAMILY WILL EXPECT YOU TO PROTECT THEM WHEN THEY NEED YOU THE MOST. SADLY, BARKING AT THE DOORBELL DOESN'T SEEM TO QUALIFY.

DON'T LET THE SMELL FOOL YOU –
SOCKS ARE NOT TASTY.

INSTRUCTION No. 32

A TOILET ROLL SHOULD BE DRAGGED THROUGH THE ENTIRE HOUSE AND THEN RIPPED TO SHREDS ONCE EVERY DAY. THIS SHOULD BE AT THE TOP OF EVERY DOGGY TO-DO LIST.

INSTRUCTION No. 33

SOME HUMANS PROCLAIM THEMSELVES TO BE 'NOT A DOG PERSON', BUT REALLY THEY'RE JUST DOG LOVERS WAITING FOR YOU TO CONVERT THEM. YOU CAN USUALLY IDENTIFY THESE PEOPLE BY THE FACT THEY'RE SITTING THE FURTHEST AWAY FROM YOU AND SQUIRMING. THESE PEOPLE ARE ESPECIALLY IN NEED OF SOME DOGGY CUDDLES, AND WOULD REALLY APPRECIATE YOU RUBBING YOUR FUR ALL OVER THEM, AND SHOWING THEM YOUR GLEAMING SMILE WITH A BIG GRIN.

INSTRUCTION No. 34

WHEN PLAYING FETCH, KEEP A CLOSE EYE ON THE HAND — IF THERE IS NO STICK, NOTHING WILL BE THROWN. DON'T BE FOOLED — JUST BECAUSE SOMEBODY MAKES THE MOTION OF THROWING A STICK, DOESN'T MEAN THERE IS A STICK. ONLY CHASE REAL STICKS, NOT PRETEND ONES. OTHERWISE YOU'LL LOOK SILLY.

INSTRUCTION No. 35

THE BEST WAY TO ENTER A SWIMMING POOL,
POND OR LAKE IS A LITTLE MOVE CALLED THE
DIVE-BOMB. NO, WAIT, THAT'S THE ONLY WAY.

INSTRUCTION No. 36

THOU SHALT POSITION THYSELF UNDER THE DINING TABLE BEFORE EVERY MEAL IS SERVED.

INSTRUCTION No. 37

BIRDS, CATS AND SQUIRRELS ARE ALL PESTS,
AND POSE HUGE DANGERS TO YOUR BELOVED
HUMANS. YOU MUST ALERT THEM TO THE
PRESENCE OF SUCH MONSTERS IN THE BACK
YARD BY RUNNING AROUND LIKE CRAZY
AND BARKING AS LOUDLY AS POSSIBLE.

SCOOTING ON YOUR BUTT. BEST ENJOYED IN
THE COMPANY OF OTHERS; BUT IT'S EVEN
MORE PLEASING ON AN EXPENSIVE CARPET
OR RUG. THE NEWER, THE BETTER.

INSTRUCTION No. 39

BONES. THEY'RE THE SKELETON OF A DEAD
THING. WHAT'S ALL THE FUSS ABOUT?
JUST LEAVE THEM BURIED.

INSTRUCTION No. 40

NEVER FEEL EMBARRASSED FOR SNIFFING A TRASH CAN, OR FOR WANTING TO GET INSIDE IT. YOU HAVE A SENSE OF SMELL 1,000 TIMES GREATER THAN HUMANS AND CAN SIMPLY APPRECIATE THE SUBTLE AROMAS MORE THAN THEM.

A DOG WITH HEALTHY TEETH IS A HEALTHY DOG.
CLEAN AND MAINTAIN YOUR OWN TEETH BY:

- CHEWING ON THE EDGES OF ALL FURNITURE.
- CHEWING ON THE PILLOWS AND FURNISHINGS THAT COVER THE FURNITURE.
- CHEWING ON ANYTHING AROUND THE HOUSE THAT LOOKS TASTY.

WHAT? I TAKE ORAL HYGIENE
VERY SERIOUSLY, THANK
YOU VERY MUCH!

INSTRUCTION No. 42

ACCOMPANYING YOUR OWNER ON A JOG:
GREAT. ACCOMPANYING YOUR OWNER
ON A BIKE RIDE? FORGET IT!

INSTRUCTION No. 43

IT'S VERY IMPORTANT TO LEARN TO SHARE
WITH YOUR HUMANS. BE GENEROUS WITH
YOUR MUDDY, CHEWED-UP TENNIS BALL
AND LET THEM ENJOY IT WITH THEIR NEXT
ROMANTIC, CANDLELIT DINNER. RIGHT IN THE
MIDDLE OF THE PLATE WHEN THEIR BACKS
ARE TURNED USUALLY DOES THE TRICK.

INSTRUCTION No. 44

YOUR OWNER, AND IN FACT MOST HUMANS, WILL BE VERY JEALOUS OF THE FACT THAT YOU CAN LICK YOURSELF CLEAN. FLAUNT THIS FACT – MAKE A SHOW OF IT.

INSTRUCTION No. 45

CARRYING STICKS TEN TIMES THE SIZE OF YOUR
OWN BODY IS ADMIRABLE, IF NOT PRACTICAL.

If you're interested in finding out more about our books, find us on Facebook at SUMMERSDALE PUBLISHERS and follow us on Twitter at @SUMMERSDALE.

WWW.SUMMERSDALE.COM